YOU AND YOUR CHILD
PARTIES

Ray Gibson
Illustrated by Sue Stitt, Simone Wood
and Graham Round

Designed by Lindy Dark
Edited by Paula Borton and Robyn Gee

Series editor: Jenny Tyler

Photography by Lesley Howling

A party is a new and exciting extension of a child's expanding world. Parents and children can have fun preparing and enjoying the occasion together, and this book provides lots of ideas for giving and for attending parties. Much of the pleasure is in the anticipation of such events, and children can be happily involved in all the preparations while learning new skills and making their own contribution.

First published in 1992 by Usborne Publishing Ltd, Usborne House, 83-85 Saffron Hill, London EC1N 8RT, England. Copyright © 1992 Usborne Publishing Ltd. The name Usborne and the device 🐝 are Trade Marks of Usborne Publishing Ltd. All rights Printed in Belgium.

Pull-out fish invitations

You will need: stiff blue paper · brightly coloured stiff paper · coloured wool · round white sticky labels · PVA glue · glue spreader · sequins · round-ended scissors

Fish

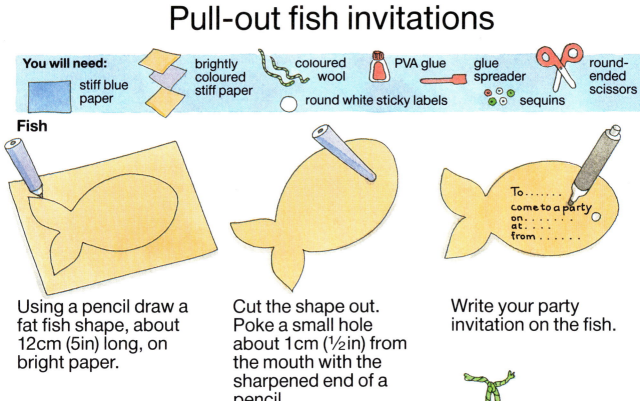

Using a pencil draw a fat fish shape, about 12cm (5in) long, on bright paper.

Cut the shape out. Poke a small hole about 1cm (½in) from the mouth with the sharpened end of a pencil.

Write your party invitation on the fish.

Other ideas

Instead of a fish, use a large motif from wrapping paper or an old greetings card. Stick onto a stiff piece of paper.

Make thankyou cards or labels by folding stiff bright paper. Decorate and add a wool tag.

Stick on gummed shapes.

Use gummed circles for balloons and draw in string.

Cut out a doily plate. Add gummed shapes for cakes. Draw on cherries.

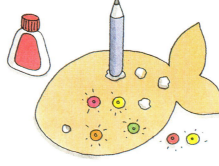

Turn the fish over and dot it with glue using the end of a pencil. Press a sequin on each glue dot.

Tie a strand of wool through the hole. Add a sticky label eye. Mark in the mouth and eye with a felt-tip pen.

Hint

Mix the glitter with sand from your sandpit for a real seashore effect on your envelope.

black felt-tip pen

pencil

old newspaper

glitter

Envelope

Fold →

Cut a piece of blue paper 35cm (14in) long 15cm (6in) wide. Fold in half, as shown, and crease the edge.

Open it out again and, working on newspaper, spread glue along the long edges. Refold the paper and press the edges together.

Draw a wavy line about 4cm (2in) from the bottom edge. Spread glue below the drawn line.

Sprinkle the area with glitter and shake off the excess.

Slide the fish into the envelope leaving the wool tag showing.

To Jess

Write your guest's name on the envelope and stick on some more sequins. Leave it to dry.

Other ways to decorate your fish

Stick on gummed paper shapes.

Print stripes using the edge of corrugated cardboard which has been pressed into paint.

Print scales using plastic 'bubble' packaging.

Stick on torn tissue, overlapping the colours.

3

Pencil-top prizes

You will need:

pencil

small piece of red felt

round-ended scissors

2 pieces green felt
9cm by 7cm (3½in by 3in)

greaseproof paper

paper clips

Freddy frog

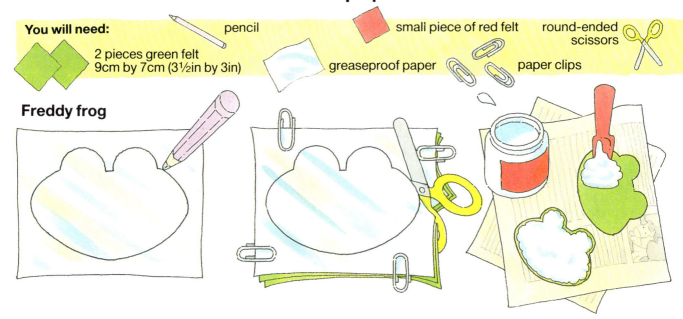

Lay greaseproof paper over the frog template*. Trace round the outline using a pencil.

Fix the tracing onto two layers of green felt using paper clips. Carefully cut out the head and then remove the paper.

Working on old newspaper, spread some glue on each cut-out shape. Spread evenly to cover right to the edges.

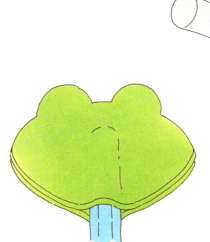

Spread glue over 2½cm (1in) of the unsharpened end of a new pencil. Lay the glued end onto one shape, as shown.

Carefully press the second shape on top and ease the edges so they meet exactly. Allow the glue to dry.

Stick on two labels for eyes, as shown. Mark in the centres with a black felt-tip pen.

old newspaper

PVA glue

glue spreader

new pencil

round white
stick-on labels

black
felt-tip pen

Give your
frog a
sleepy look.

Add a wide mouth and
nostrils. Glue on a
bow-tie cut from a
scrap of red felt.

Glue on some
felt buttons.

Other ideas to try

Badge

Use sticking
plaster to fix a
safety pin onto a
single layer felt
face.

Hairband

Glue a single layer
felt face, slightly
off-centre, onto a
smooth hairband.

Finger puppet

Leave an unglued
area in the centre
of the shape big
enough to insert a
finger.

Other animal pencil-tops

Cat

Use grey felt for
a cat pencil top*.
Add green felt for the
eyes and a pink
felt nose. Draw
in face as shown.

Rabbit

Make a rabbit face out
of white felt*. Use pink
felt for the nose and
inner ears. Draw in the
face with a black felt-
tip pen.

Duck

Cut out a yellow
felt face using
the duck
template*. Glue
on an orange beak
and use labels for
eyes and mark
as shown.

Pig

Use pink felt for a pig*.
Glue on ears and a
snout. Use half labels for
eyes. Mark in the eyes
and nose with a felt-tip
pen.

Balloon people

You will need: greaseproof paper · small balloons · thin cardboard · paper clips · pencil · round-ended scissors

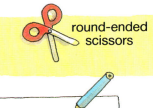

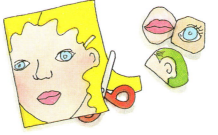

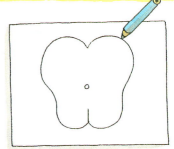

Blow up some balloons and knot the ends. Don't make them too full.

Cut some eyes, noses and ears from old magazines.

Lay some greaseproof paper over the balloon feet template* and, using a pencil, carefully trace the shape.

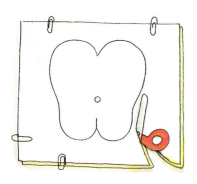

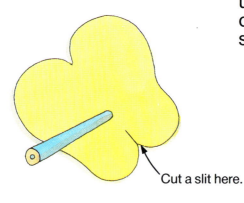

Cut a slit here.

Secure the tracing onto a piece of cardboard with paper clips and cut out the feet.

Poke a hole, as marked, using the sharpened end of a pencil.

Push the knotted end of a balloon through the hole.

Hints

● Keep balloons fairly small so they will balance easily on the feet, and be less likely to burst.

● It can be easier to apply glue directly onto the balloon, rather than pasting the paper and wool.

● Guests arriving at a party can decorate their own balloon. Prepare the feet in advance. To make lots of feet use the first pair as a pattern to draw round.

● To pop balloons without a bang, stick on a small piece of sticky tape and prick with a pin.

Stretch the knot backwards through the slit, as shown.

See templates on pages 30-31.

PVA glue   glue spreader   cotton wool

sticky tape   old magazines   wool strands

Tape the knot onto the back of the balloon.

Stand the balloon on its feet. Decorate it with glued-on eyes, nose and mouth . Glue on cotton wool and wool strands for hair .

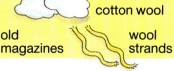

Warning

Never allow children to put bits of burst balloon near their mouths or noses. This can cause suffocation.

You can colour in the feet.

Clown take-home picture

Provide lots of thick felt-tip pens and sheets of paper. Draw and colour large clown faces. Poke a hole in the centre with the sharpened end of a pencil. Push the knotted end of a slightly inflated red balloon through the hole to make a shiny nose. Secure the knot at the back with sticky tape.

Balloon nose

Balloon games

Throw two or three balloons into the air and see how long you can keep them up.

Give everyone a long and a round balloon. They must try and 'bat' a round balloon into a cardboard box turned on its side. First one in is the winner. Winners are easier to identify if you match the colours of the 'bat' and 'ball'.

Other ideas

Stick gummed paper shapes onto balloons to decorate.

Use balloons as party invitations. Attach an uninflated balloon to the front of a card with double-sided sticky tape. Write 'You and your balloon are invited to . . .'

Robbie
You and your balloon are invited to a party.

Crocodile mosaic cake

You will need: 75g (3oz) margarine • 60g (2½oz) self-raising flour • 15g (¾oz) cocoa powder • 75g (3oz) caster sugar • 2 small eggs • icing sugar • yellow and green food colouring*

large mixing bowl • wooden spoon • tea towel • sieve • oven gloves • cooling rack • 3 small bowls • teaspoons • large baking tray • sticky tape • 1 pack of petit four cases

Sift both the cocoa and the flour into a small bowl.

In a large bowl, beat the margarine and sugar until light and fluffy. Stand the bowl on a tea towel to prevent it slipping.

Beat the eggs into the mixture, one at a time, adding a little flour and cocoa with each.

Add the remaining flour and cocoa to the mixture. Stir well.

Place the petit four cases on a baking tray. Half fill them with the cake mixture.

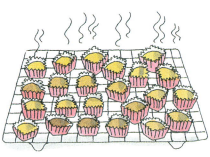

Bake the cakes in a pre-heated oven for 15 to 20 minutes, or until the centres feel springy. Place them on a cooling rack.

Sift a little icing sugar, enough for two cakes, into a bowl. Mix it with a few drops of water.

Add a very small amount of yellow food colouring to the icing and mix it well.

In another bowl, mix a larger amount of green icing for the remaining cakes.

8   * You can buy natural food colours from health food stores.

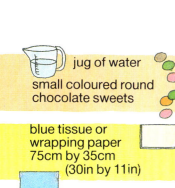

jug of water

small coloured round chocolate sweets

blue tissue or wrapping paper 75cm by 35cm (30in by 11in)

piece of cardboard 70cm by 30cm (27in by 11in)

Other ideas

Use different coloured icing and arrange patterns of cakes on plates.

Try other shapes such as a striped snake, a large flower or a big fish.

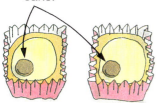

Press a brown sweet near the bottom of each cake.

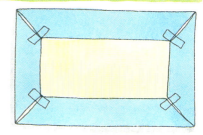

Place some yellow icing onto two cakes and spread with a teaspoon.

Ice the remaining cakes and press coloured sweets onto the centre of each.

For the background, cover a large piece of cardboard with blue tissue paper and tape it at the back.

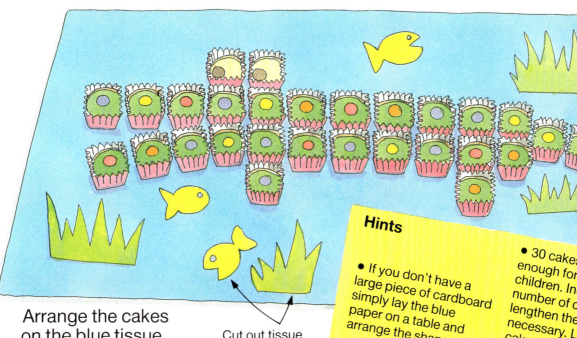

Arrange the cakes on the blue tissue paper in a crocodile shape, as shown.

Cut out tissue paper reeds and fish to decorate the 'river'.

Hints

• If you don't have a large piece of cardboard simply lay the blue paper on a table and arrange the shape.

• 30 cakes will be enough for about 10 children. Increase the number of cakes and lengthen the crocodile if necessary. Leftover cakes can go in party take-home bags.

Octopus tablecloth

You will need: thick water-based paints in various colours old newspaper / large paper plates (or old plates) 1 per colour / fat drinking straw / pieces of thick cotton or wool cloth / plastic fork

Printing pads

Place a piece of thick cloth on an old plate. Pour on a good quantity of paint.

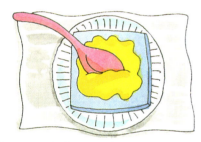

Spread the paint evenly over the pad using the back of a spoon. Make one pad for each colour.

Octopus

Press one hand onto the printing pad with fingers spread. Press firmly onto the tablecloth.

When dry, stick on adhesive round labels for eyes and mark in the centres with black felt-tip pen.

Boulders

Cut a potato in half. Score the cut surface by drawing the prongs of a fork firmly across. Overlap the boulders in different colours.

Lay the tablecloth on a flat surface over old newspaper.

Hints
• You can print well on sheets of tissue paper. Tape them together lightly to make a big cloth.

• Rock the hand or vegetable to ensure even printing. Press firmly on the paper.

Carefully wash and dry hands after printing. Protect clothing with aprons.

Sea plants

Cut a brussels sprout from top to bottom and use it to make prints.

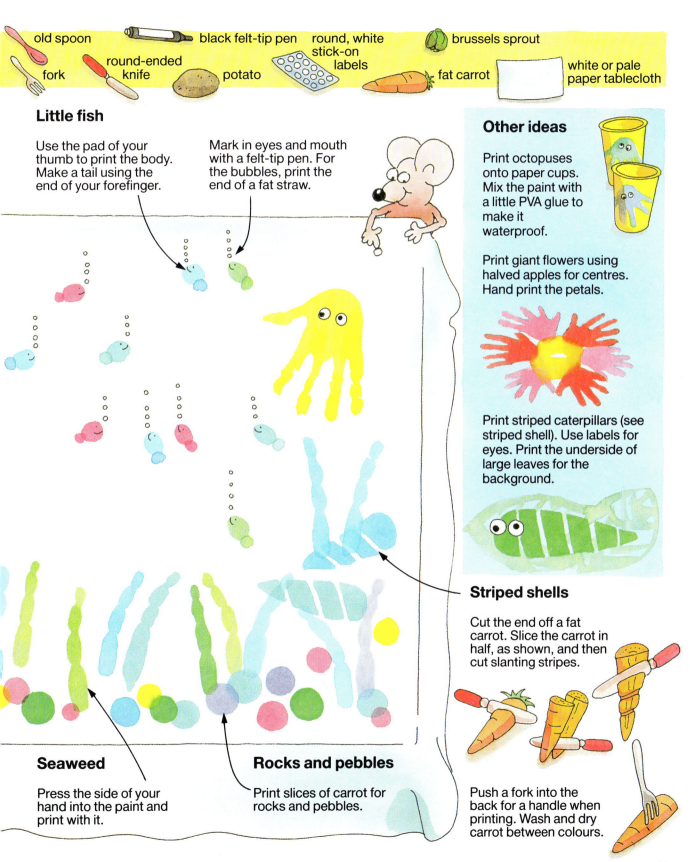

old spoon

fork

round-ended knife

black felt-tip pen

potato

round, white stick-on labels

brussels sprout

fat carrot

white or pale paper tablecloth

Little fish

Use the pad of your thumb to print the body. Make a tail using the end of your forefinger.

Mark in eyes and mouth with a felt-tip pen. For the bubbles, print the end of a fat straw.

Other ideas

Print octopuses onto paper cups. Mix the paint with a little PVA glue to make it waterproof.

Print giant flowers using halved apples for centres. Hand print the petals.

Print striped caterpillars (see striped shell). Use labels for eyes. Print the underside of large leaves for the background.

Striped shells

Cut the end off a fat carrot. Slice the carrot in half, as shown, and then cut slanting stripes.

Seaweed

Press the side of your hand into the paint and print with it.

Rocks and pebbles

Print slices of carrot for rocks and pebbles.

Push a fork into the back for a handle when printing. Wash and dry carrot between colours.

11

Jumping teddy

You will need: pencil · ruler · plastic or paper cup · glue spreader · 2 small and 1 large black button · piece of stiff yellow paper 40cm by 46cm (16in by 18in) · saucer · round-ended scissors · PVA glue · drawing pin

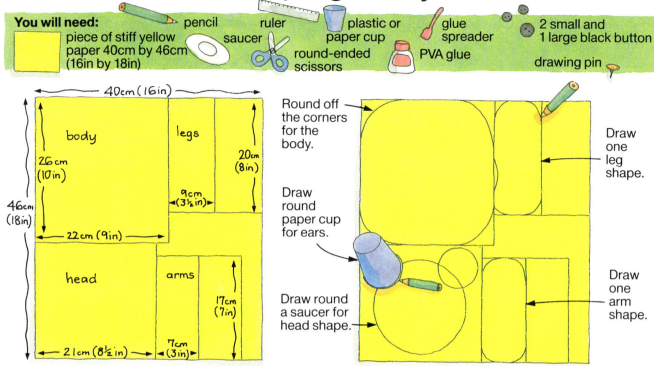

Using a pencil and ruler, measure and draw rectangles on stiff yellow paper.

Draw body shapes, as shown. Cut out all the rectangles and the head and body shapes.

Round off the corners for the body.

Draw round paper cup for ears.

Draw round a saucer for head shape.

Draw one leg shape.

Draw one arm shape.

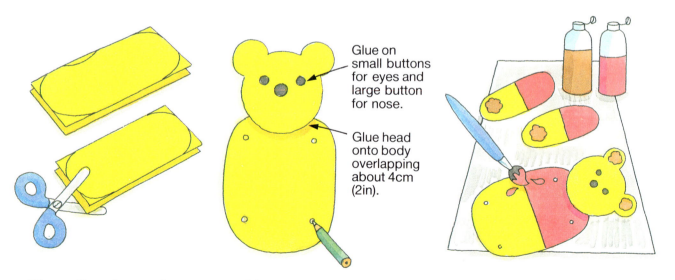

Place the drawn leg over the other leg piece. Cut out two legs. Do the same for the arms.

Glue on the head and buttons and leave to dry. Poke holes in the body with a sharp pencil point.

Glue on small buttons for eyes and large button for nose.

Glue head onto body overlapping about 4cm (2in).

Working on newspaper, paint the paws and inside of the ears brown. Paint a red T-shirt on the arms and the body.

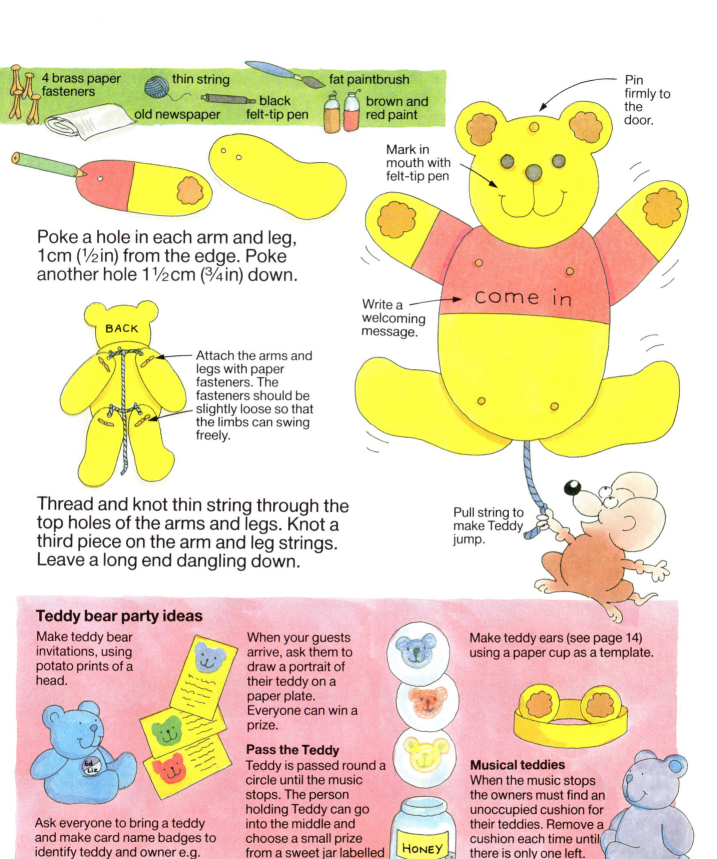

4 brass paper fasteners

thin string

fat paintbrush

old newspaper

black felt-tip pen

brown and red paint

Pin firmly to the door.

Mark in mouth with felt-tip pen

Write a welcoming message.

come in

Poke a hole in each arm and leg, 1cm (½in) from the edge. Poke another hole 1½cm (¾in) down.

BACK

Attach the arms and legs with paper fasteners. The fasteners should be slightly loose so that the limbs can swing freely.

Thread and knot thin string through the top holes of the arms and legs. Knot a third piece on the arm and leg strings. Leave a long end dangling down.

Pull string to make Teddy jump.

Teddy bear party ideas

Make teddy bear invitations, using potato prints of a head.

Ask everyone to bring a teddy and make card name badges to identify teddy and owner e.g. Edward-Eliza. Pin onto the bears.

When your guests arrive, ask them to draw a portrait of their teddy on a paper plate. Everyone can win a prize.

Pass the Teddy

Teddy is passed round a circle until the music stops. The person holding Teddy can go into the middle and choose a small prize from a sweet jar labelled HONEY.

HONEY

Make teddy ears (see page 14) using a paper cup as a template.

Musical teddies

When the music stops the owners must find an unoccupied cushion for their teddies. Remove a cushion each time until there is only one left.

Mouse ears

You will need:
2 squares of stiff grey paper 14cm by 14cm (5½in by 5½in)

greaseproof paper

2 squares pink paper 10cm by 10cm (4in by 4in)

strip of stiff grey paper 55cm by 10cm (22in by 4in)

pencil

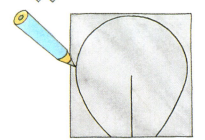

Lay some greaseproof paper on the mouse ear template*. Trace the outline and centre line with a pencil.

Line up the tracing with two grey paper squares and secure it with paper clips. Cut along all the drawn lines carefully, then remove the tracing.

Carefully trace the ear centres from the template*. Using pink paper, cut them out in the same way as the outer ears.

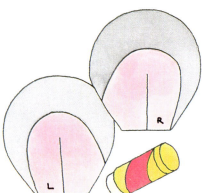

Turn the top ear centre over and glue both centres to the ears, matching corners and centre lines. Label them left and right.

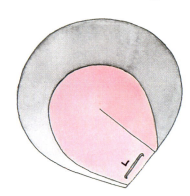

Lift the left side of the left ear and overlap onto the right side. Match the corners and staple, as shown.

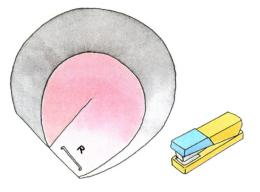

Lift the right side of the right ear and overlap onto the left side. Match the corners and staple at the base.

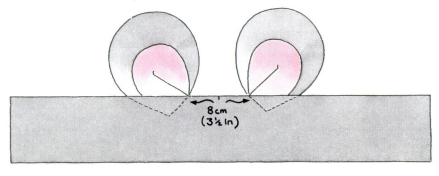

8cm (3½in)

Mark the centre of the paper strip. Staple left and right ears at each side 8cm (3½in) apart.

round-ended scissors | stapler | sticky tape | glue stick | paper clips | ruler

Fold the band over itself to hide the staples. Fit the band round the head and secure it with paper clips.

To prevent staples catching on hair cover the staples at the back with sticky tape.

Fold over

Using face paints, draw on a round black nose and whiskers.

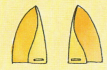

Cat ears

Cut out two cat ears from orange paper using the cat ears template*. Turn in, but do not fold, the inner corners 3cm (1½in). Staple at the base.

Attach the ears to an orange paper band 6cm (2½in) apart. Decorate with felt-tip pens.

Cat face

Draw on a pink triangular nose, add whiskers and orange and brown stripes.

Pig

Using pink paper, cut two ears from the cat ears template*. Turn in both bottom corners and staple as for the cat ears.

Draw on a snout, or use an egg box section painted pink with two drawn nose holes. Attach round the head with fine elastic.

Dog

Cut two long floppy ears allowing them to hang down over the headband.

Draw on a black patch eye, nose and whiskers.

Sheep

Cut two floppy black ears. Attach them to a white headband with cotton wool stuck onto it.

Draw on a black nose.

Pirate fancy dress

You will need:  white paper  string  glue stick  thin cardboard 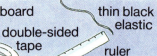 thin black elastic

black paper 58cm by 37cm (23in by 15in) round-ended scissors black felt-tip pen kitchen foil double-sided tape ruler sticky tape

Pirate's hat

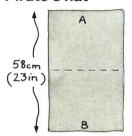

Fold the piece of black paper so that edge A meets edge B exactly.

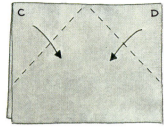

Now fold the points marked C and D so they meet in the centre.

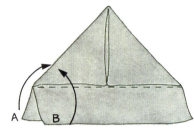

Fold up the edges B and A on either side to complete the hat.

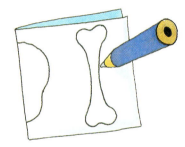

Fold a white piece of paper in half. Draw half a skull and a bone.

Cut out the skull and crossbones. Draw in the skull's face with a black felt-tip pen.

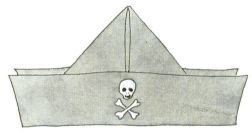

Glue the shapes onto the front of your hat, like this.

Dagger

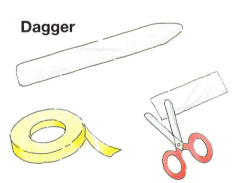

Cut out a rounded blade and handle from thin cardboard. Cover both pieces with kitchen foil using tape.

Stick on the handle, as shown, with double-sided tape. Wind some string round the handle and tape the ends.

Treasure map

Tear round a piece of unlined white paper. Soak in cold tea for a few minutes. Hang it up to dry. Use brown felt-tip pen to draw a treasure map. Roll it up loosely and tie it with a red ribbon.

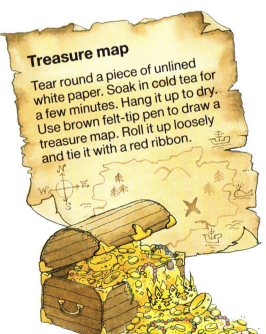

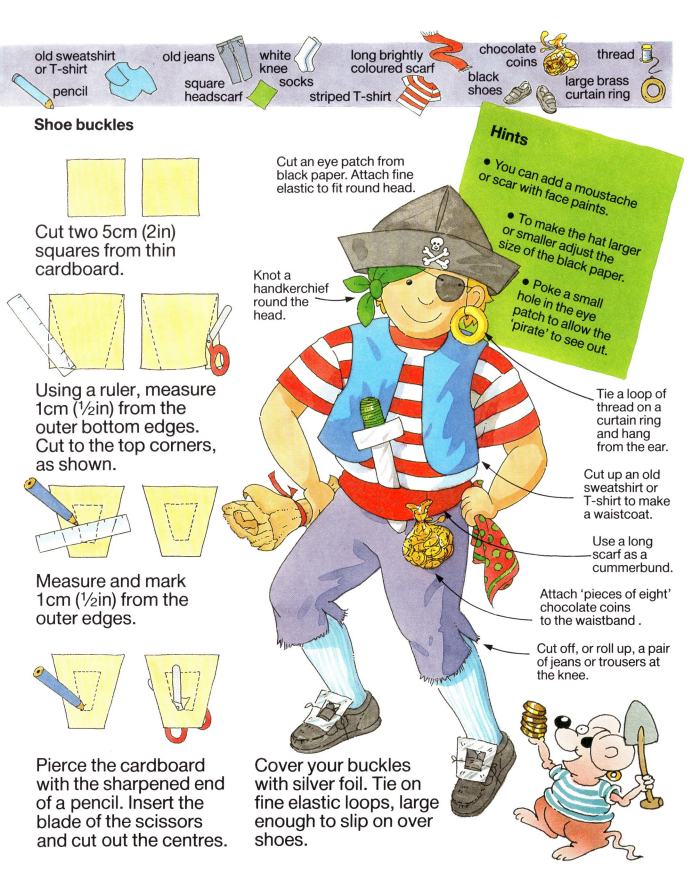

old sweatshirt or T-shirt

pencil

old jeans

square headscarf

white knee socks

striped T-shirt

long brightly coloured scarf

black shoes

chocolate coins

large brass curtain ring

thread

Shoe buckles

Cut two 5cm (2in) squares from thin cardboard.

Using a ruler, measure 1cm (½in) from the outer bottom edges. Cut to the top corners, as shown.

Measure and mark 1cm (½in) from the outer edges.

Pierce the cardboard with the sharpened end of a pencil. Insert the blade of the scissors and cut out the centres.

Cover your buckles with silver foil. Tie on fine elastic loops, large enough to slip on over shoes.

Cut an eye patch from black paper. Attach fine elastic to fit round head.

Knot a handkerchief round the head.

Hints

● You can add a moustache or scar with face paints.

● To make the hat larger or smaller adjust the size of the black paper.

● Poke a small hole in the eye patch to allow the 'pirate' to see out.

Tie a loop of thread on a curtain ring and hang from the ear.

Cut up an old sweatshirt or T-shirt to make a waistcoat.

Use a long scarf as a cummerbund.

Attach 'pieces of eight' chocolate coins to the waistband.

Cut off, or roll up, a pair of jeans or trousers at the knee.

Little witch

You will need: tape measure • sticky tape • ribbon • pencil • large sheet of stiff black paper • 2 black plastic bin liners at least 90cm (35in) long • scissors • PVA glue • kitchen foil • string • glue spreader • dinner plate

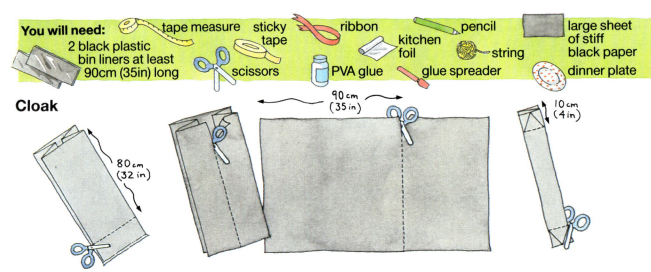

Cloak

With the open end of a bin liner at the top, cut a wide tube 80cm (32in) deep. Keep the remaining piece.

Cut the top layer and open it out to make a wide strip. Trim the strip to 90cm (35in) wide.

Fold the strip in half widthways three times. Cut the top and bottom into points about 10cm (4in) deep.

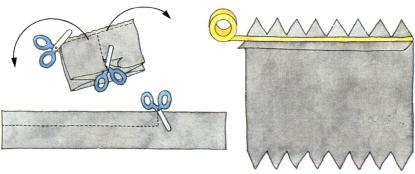
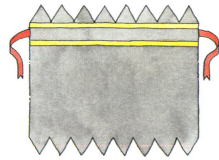

From the remaining piece of bin liner cut a band, as shown, 90cm (35in) long and 8cm (3in) wide.

Open out the folded strip and lay the band over the top of the cloak. Tape along the top edge.

Lay a ribbon between the cloak and the band. Tape down the bottom edge. Draw up the ribbon to gather the neck edge.

Other cloak ideas

Vampire

Leave top edge uncut to make a stiff, stand-up collar.

Superman or woman

Leave uncut.

Glue a foil motif on the back.

Leave uncut.

Magician

Leave uncut.

Glue on red crêpe paper lining (see 'Top hat' on the opposite page).

Leave uncut.

tea plate
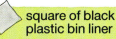 square of black plastic bin liner
lump of playdough
thin black elastic
 drawing pin
tissue
round white sticky labels

Hint

If the hat is too big, pad the inside with glued-on strips of foam rubber or cotton wadding.

Hat

Place a dinner plate on a sheet of black paper. Draw round it with a pencil. Cut out the circle.

Place a small tea plate on the centre of the circle. Draw round it.

Poke a hole in the centre of the paper using a pencil point. Make cuts to the drawn circle, as shown.

Insert the blade of the scissors.

Use the tea plate as a guide to size.

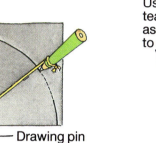

— Drawing pin

Tie a piece of string 26-29cm (10-12in) long to a pencil. Attach to the paper with a drawing pin and draw a semicircle. Cut it out.

Bend the edges to make a cone. Secure inside and out with sticky tape.

Spread glue onto the centre of the brim. Bend the points upwards.

Poke holes in the cone and attach elastic.

Place the points of the brim inside the cone and press firmly. When the glue is dry, strengthen with tape.

Gather up the ribbon.

Glue on kitchen foil stars and moons.

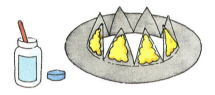
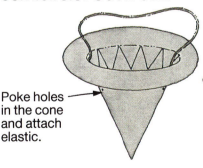

Other hat ideas

Top hat
Attach a cylinder to the brim instead of a cone. Add ribbon. Use for a posh man or a magician.

Pierrot
Use white paper for the cone. Glue on snipped black wool for pom–poms.

Wizard
Use a black or purple cone and wear witch's cloak.

Princess
Use a gold-coloured cone. Snip a hole in the top. Tape on net curtain for a veil. Glue on wine gum jewels.

Continued on next page.

19

black felt-tip pen — face paints — book — wrapping paper — black leotard or black T-shirt — stick-on stars — raffia or crêpe paper — black pipe cleaners — dowelling — long twigs

Spider

Crumple a tissue around a lump of playdough and wrap it in a square of bin liner plastic.

Tape the bottom and add small round sticky labels for eyes. Mark in eye centres with felt-tip pen.

Bend four black pipe cleaners and tape to the body, as shown. Attach fine black elastic with sticky tape.

Warning

Do not leave children alone with plastic bags lying around. Explain the dangers of putting plastic near their faces.

Paint face with pale green face paint. Add red round eyes.

Glue raffia or snipped crêpe paper 'hair' to the inside of the brim.

Wear a black T-shirt or leotard under the dress.

Cut a length of dowelling for a broom handle. Tie on some long twigs or raffia.

Tape another spider to the brim.

Use a strip of bin liner for a belt.

Cover a book with wrapping paper. Write 'SPELLS' in large letters and decorate with stick-on stars.

For the dress, cut arm and neck holes out of a black bin liner. Trim the bottom to fit and cut a jagged edge. Decorate with foil stars and moons.

Loop spider elastic round the wrist.

For silver buckles see page 17.

20

Other dressing-up ideas

Waitress

Stick half a doily onto a strip of stiff white paper. Secure with paper clips at the back.

Lipstick

Doily 'collar' and 'cuffs'.

Fold a card and stick food pictures inside.

Tape a small and large doily together for the apron. Add a white ribbon.

Tie on a notebook and pencil.

Use a polystyrene pizza base as a tray. Glue on a paper cup with straw. Fill small cake cases with breakfast cereal mixed with PVA glue. Paint the 'cakes' brown and glue onto tray.

Chef

Tape the edges of a circle of white crêpe paper to the inside of a white paper band.

Dust the face with flour.

Apron

Small rolling pin

Pastry brush

Wooden spoon

For the sausages, stuff the legs of old tights and tie at intervals with thread.

Spider

Black balaclava

You can glue on silver foil stripes.

Stuff the legs of old black tights and attach with a safety pin.

Black gloves

Black jumper

Suspend 'legs' from strong black thread.

Black tights

Black plimsolls

Clown

Slippers

Cut-down too-large trousers.

Cotton patches

Braces

For the buttons, cut off the bottoms of paper cups. Poke in holes and sew lightly onto T-shirt.

Scarf 'bow-tie'

Nose made of an egg carton section painted red. Tie on with elastic.

Rubber bands keep gloves on.

21

Fishing game

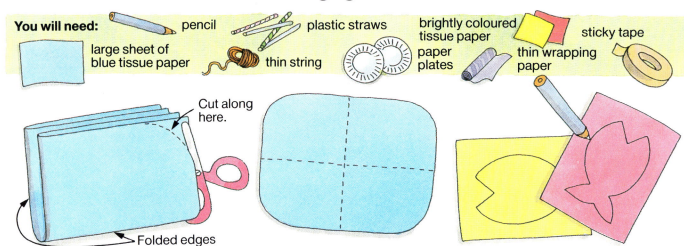
Fold a sheet of blue tissue paper into four. Round off the outer corner with scissors, as shown.

Open it and smooth it out on the floor. This is your pond.

On pieces of tissue paper and wrapping paper draw large, simple fish shapes about 15cm (6in) long. You will need 15 to 20 fishes.

Cut out the shapes neatly. Decorate your fish with felt-tip pens.

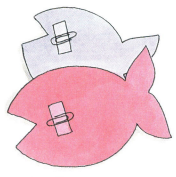

Turn the fish shapes over. Place a paper clip near the mouth of each fish. Secure the paper clips with sticky tape.

Hints

• Use thin wrapping paper or the magnet won't pick up the fish.

• Cut out a number of fish at a time by cutting through several layers of paper.

• Adjust the rod according to the height of the child by winding or unwinding the string round the straw.

• To store the game wind the string round each straw and fold the pond. Keep all the pieces in a flat box.

Flapping fish game

Cut out large tissue paper fish shapes about 25cm (10in) long. Decorate them with felt-tip pens. Race your fish by blowing them or flapping them with rolled-up newspaper. Use a wool strand as a starting line.

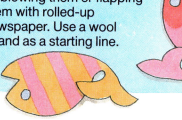

22

magnetic shapes
(letters, numbers
or any other
fridge magnets)

round-ended
scissors

felt-tip
pens

metal
paper clips

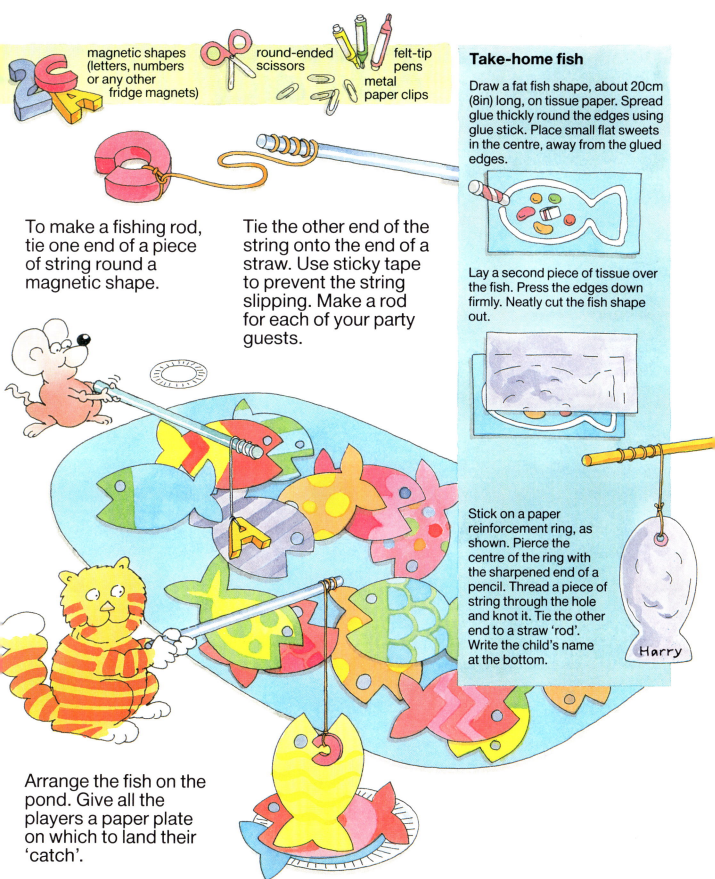

To make a fishing rod, tie one end of a piece of string round a magnetic shape.

Tie the other end of the string onto the end of a straw. Use sticky tape to prevent the string slipping. Make a rod for each of your party guests.

Take-home fish

Draw a fat fish shape, about 20cm (8in) long, on tissue paper. Spread glue thickly round the edges using glue stick. Place small flat sweets in the centre, away from the glued edges.

Lay a second piece of tissue over the fish. Press the edges down firmly. Neatly cut the fish shape out.

Stick on a paper reinforcement ring, as shown. Pierce the centre of the ring with the sharpened end of a pencil. Thread a piece of string through the hole and knot it. Tie the other end to a straw 'rod'. Write the child's name at the bottom.

Harry

Arrange the fish on the pond. Give all the players a paper plate on which to land their 'catch'.

Buzzing bees game

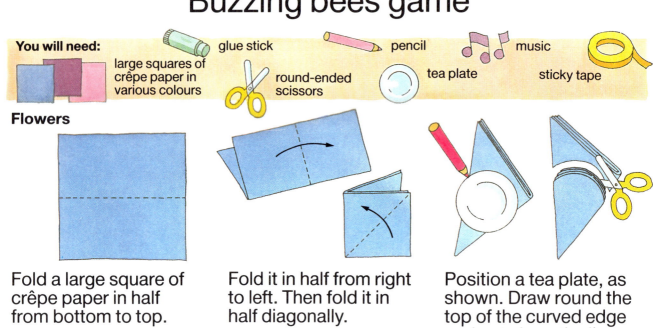

You will need: glue stick · large squares of crêpe paper in various colours · round-ended scissors · pencil · tea plate · music · sticky tape

Flowers

Fold a large square of crêpe paper in half from bottom to top.

Fold it in half from right to left. Then fold it in half diagonally.

Position a tea plate, as shown. Draw round the top of the curved edge and cut along the line. Open out the flower.

Buzz! Buzz!

Players must take off their shoes.

Make a centre by drawing round a tea plate and cutting out the shape. Glue it on.

Make a flower for each 'bee'.

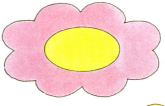

Tape the flowers lightly to the floor.

How to play the game

The players dance to music until it stops. They then buzz to a flower. Remove one flower each time, so that one player will be out. The winner is queen bee.

Hints for playing games

- Taped music is best for games as it is easily controlled.

- Have a toy corner for children who dislike games. Ask shy children to set up games and give out prizes.

- Alternate noisy games with quiet ones.

- Have one or two practice runs for each game.

- Keep a few extra prizes for emergencies.

- Small children can often get upset if they are 'out' in a game. Allow them to continue to play.

Poor piggy

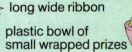

Piggy

Tie rubber bands round two corners of the pillowcase. Draw on eyes and a snout with pink felt-tip pen or paint.

Fit a pillow inside the pillowcase. Gather in the 'neck' with a wide ribbon

How to play the game

Pass poor piggy round in a circle until the music stops. Whoever is holding poor piggy calls out 'oink oink' and collects a prize from the bowl in the centre.

Hint

Make sure the person in charge of the music can see all the players clearly so that every child 'wins' a prize.

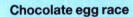

Other games to play

Adapt the buzzing bees game for a theme party. Cut out islands for pirates to jump on, or honey pots for teddy bears.

Wool gathering

Players find pieces of wool hidden round a room while music plays. When the music stops, the child with most pieces gives out a sweet 'prize' to the others.

Chocolate egg race

Small chocolate eggs, placed in a plastic bowl, are scooped up with plastic teaspoons and raced to woolly hat nests. When the music stops, the nest with most eggs wins. This can be a team game.

Ping-pong ball race

Using straws, race ping-pong balls by blowing them along the floor into an upturned box 'goal'. No hands allowed.

Miming games

One player mimes an animal while the others guess. Try other themes, such as circus performers or sports.

Outdoor party fun

You will need:  4 large sturdy cardboard boxes — breadknife — old washing line or fine rope — ball-point pen — water-based paints — small household paintbrushes — sharp scissors — old or paper plates — ruler

Crawl-through tunnel

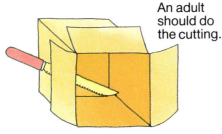

An adult should do the cutting.

Using a breadknife, cut off the top and bottom flaps of the boxes. Discard the flaps.

Lay the boxes on one wide side. Using a ball-point pen, poke holes 15cm (6in) apart

on the top edges and 5cm (2in) from the outside edges.

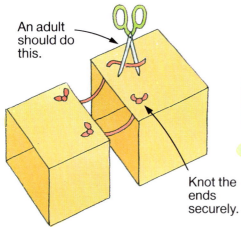

An adult should do this.

Knot the ends securely.

Link the boxes by threading rope through the holes. Use sharp scissors to cut the rope. The ends should be left long enough to knot.

Hint

Keep the gaps between the boxes narrow to avoid heads getting caught.

Pour some paint onto old or paper plates. Paint bold, bright designs on the boxes using household paintbrushes.

Cut some peepholes out of the sides and tops of the boxes.

Giant caterpillar

You could paint the tunnel like a giant caterpillar. Tape on paper 'teeth' which will eat the guests.

Other ideas

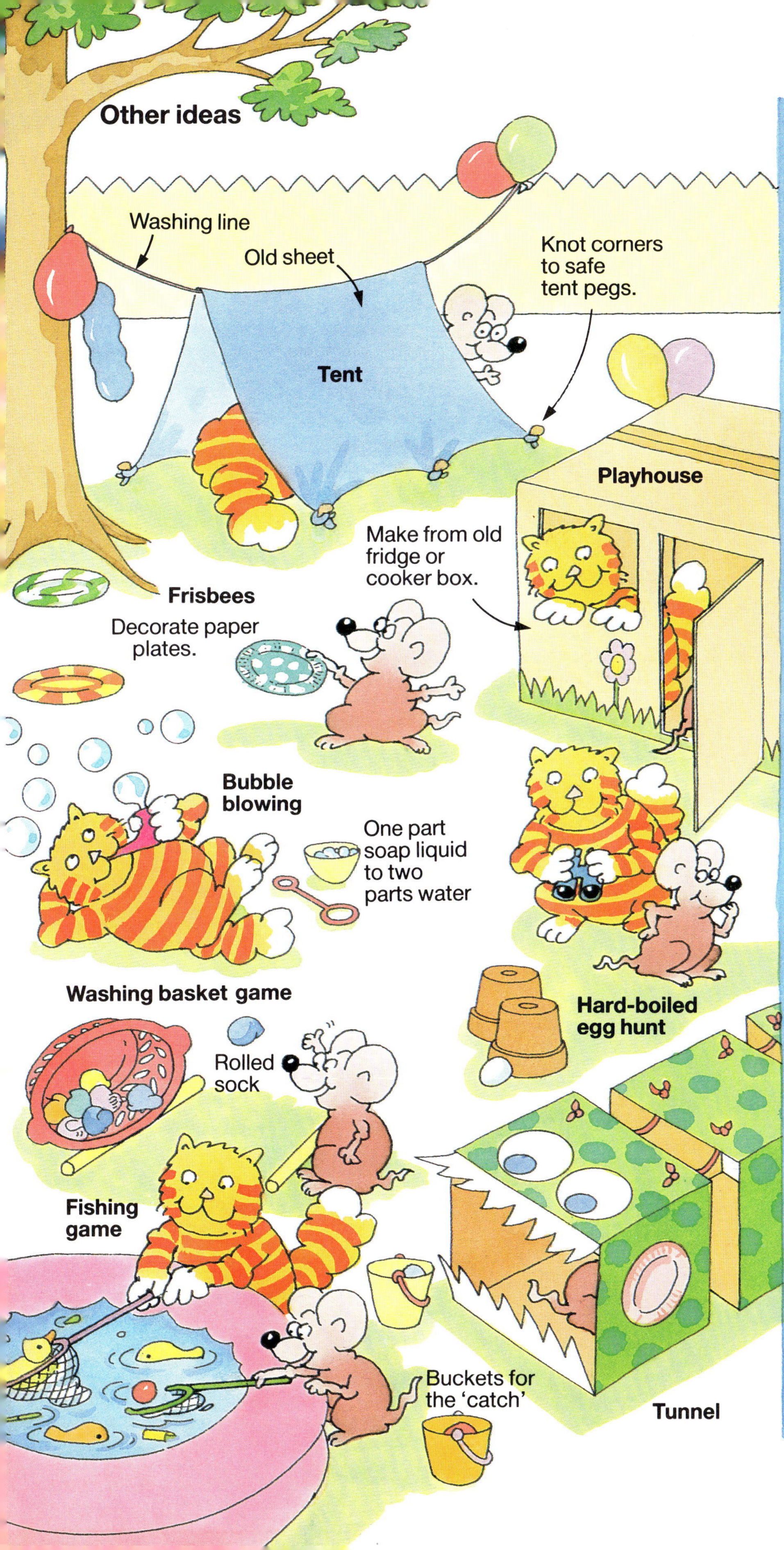

Washing line

Old sheet

Knot corners to safe tent pegs.

Tent

Playhouse

Make from old fridge or cooker box.

Frisbees

Decorate paper plates.

Bubble blowing

One part soap liquid to two parts water

Hard-boiled egg hunt

Washing basket game

Rolled sock

Fishing game

Buckets for the 'catch'

Tunnel

Mice and cheese lucky dip

You will need: black felt-tip pen

pieces of stiff grey paper 11cm by 6cm (4½in by 2½in)

round-ended scissors

pieces of stiff pink paper 2cm by 5cm (¾in by 2in)

small presents

ruler

strands of coloured wool 50cm (20in) long

Mouse

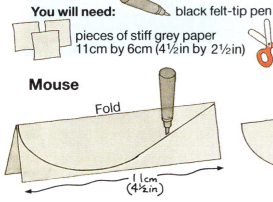

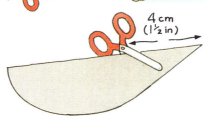

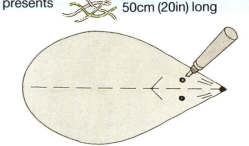

Fold the grey paper in half, and draw a shape, as shown, with a felt-tip pen.

Cut out the shape. Make a slanting cut 1cm (½in) deep, 4cm (1½in) from the pointed end.

Open the mouse out flat. Mark in the eyes, nose and whiskers with a black felt-tip pen.

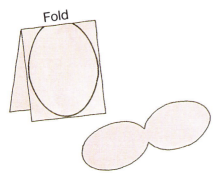

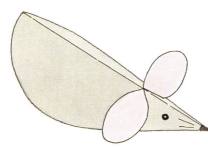

Fold the pink paper, as shown. Draw and cut out the ears, leaving them joined at the fold.

Fold the mouse again and stand it upright. Then slot the ears into the cut on the mouse's back.

Other ideas

Make a Christmas chimney pot. Cut the flaps off a tall box and cover it with brown paper. Paint or, using a sponge, print red bricks. Glue on cotton wool snow and sprinkle with glitter.

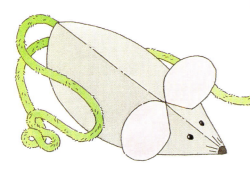

Tape one end of the wool to the inside top of the mouse's body.

Tape a small wrapped present to the other end of the wool. Make one mouse per guest.

For very young children, cover a large box with bright paper. Fill with wrapped presents mixed among lots of small soft toys.

Wrap a large box to look like a parcel. Paint on a stamp. Cut a hole in the side and fill it with presents.

oblong cardboard box about 40cm by 30cm (16in by 12in)

small household paintbrush

thick yellow paint

breadknife

ball-point pen

newspaper

paper or old plate

orange felt-tip pen

saucer

sticky tape

Cheese

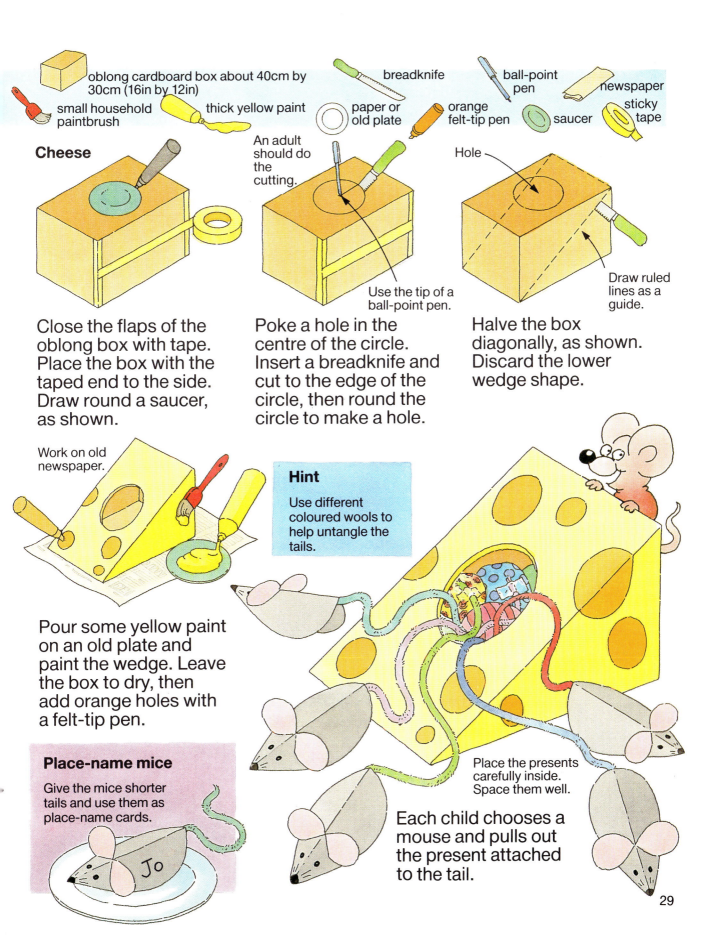

An adult should do the cutting.

Use the tip of a ball-point pen.

Hole

Draw ruled lines as a guide.

Close the flaps of the oblong box with tape. Place the box with the taped end to the side. Draw round a saucer, as shown.

Poke a hole in the centre of the circle. Insert a breadknife and cut to the edge of the circle, then round the circle to make a hole.

Halve the box diagonally, as shown. Discard the lower wedge shape.

Work on old newspaper.

Hint

Use different coloured wools to help untangle the tails.

Pour some yellow paint on an old plate and paint the wedge. Leave the box to dry, then add orange holes with a felt-tip pen.

Place-name mice

Give the mice shorter tails and use them as place-name cards.

Jo

Place the presents carefully inside. Space them well.

Each child chooses a mouse and pulls out the present attached to the tail.

29

Templates

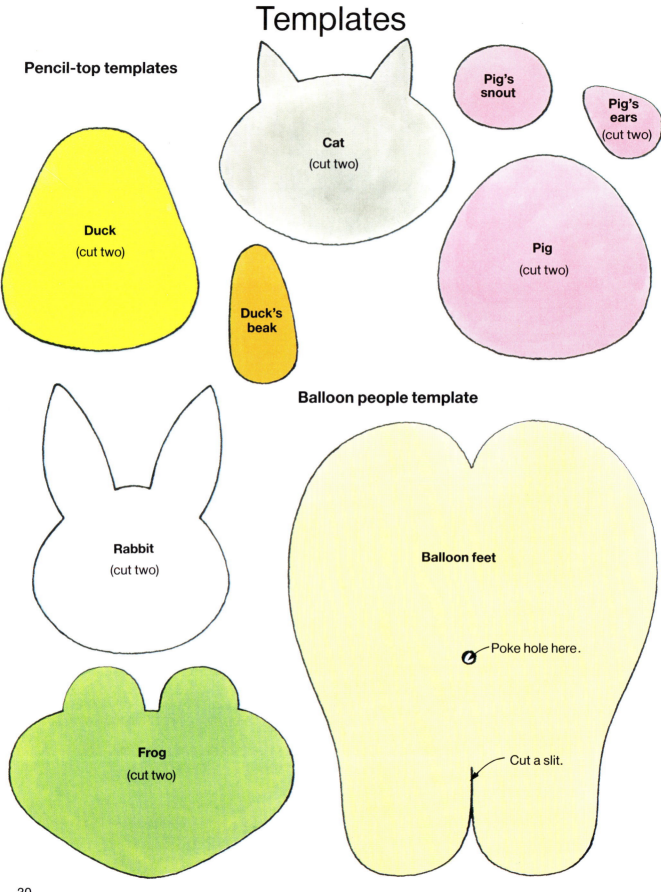

Pencil-top templates

Duck
(cut two)

Cat
(cut two)

Pig's snout

Pig's ears
(cut two)

Pig
(cut two)

Duck's beak

Rabbit
(cut two)

Balloon people template

Balloon feet

Poke hole here.

Cut a slit.

Frog
(cut two)

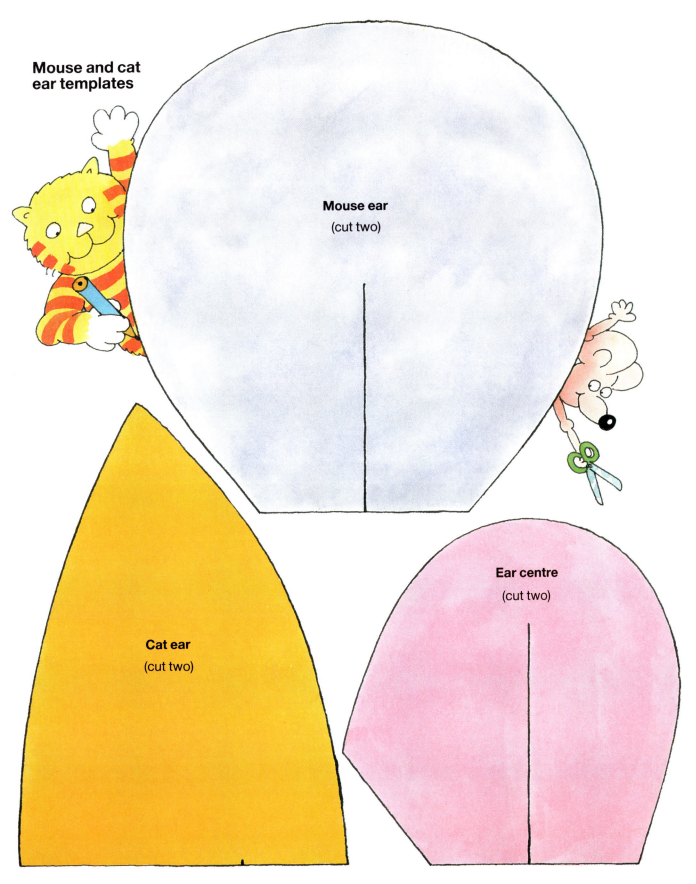

Mouse and cat ear templates

Mouse ear
(cut two)

Cat ear
(cut two)

Ear centre
(cut two)

31

Parents' notes

Party hints

Number of guests

Large numbers of people can overwhelm small children, especially if they are unfamiliar with all the guests and adults present. A small number of close friends can often work better. If there are more than one or two 'new' children, it can be a good idea to provide name badges. These could be sent with the party invitations.

Games

If you have room, provide a selection of toys in a small corner for children who find it difficult joining in games. Shy children can also be encouraged to hand out sweets or prizes, and help to set up the games.

Alternate noisy games with quiet ones and end the party with a 'keeping still' or 'lying on the floor' game.

Safety

It is important to make sure the party area is safe. Make sure that outside gates are secure and that rooms you wish to be undisturbed are locked and keys removed. These places could act as stores for delicate or dangerous objects, or furniture which has been cleared to create space.

Make sure outside ponds or paddling pools are drained or covered, and garden tools are locked away. Have a small first-aid kit handy.

Food

Don't make food too elaborate, except, perhaps, for a birthday cake which your child may like to help you make.

You can avoid 'one bite' leftovers by keeping the food small. Bowls of finger foods, such as crisps and cut-up sausages; tiny sandwiches and small cakes in petit four cases make ideal party fare. You could also provide individual juice cartons to avoid spills.

Materials

The specific things you will need for each project are listed at the top of each page. Below is some general advice on equipment and materials.

Scissors should be round-ended. If sharp ones are needed remember to place them safely out of reach. Cut roughly round the shape you want and then it will be easier to neaten the cut edge.

Paper. Packs of coloured play paper can be bought quite cheaply. You can also use wrapping paper or wallpaper but make sure it is a suitable thickness for your project. Breakfast cereal boxes make a good source of thin cardboard.

Glue sticks are clean to use, and they do not cause wrinkling on thin paper such as tissue.

PVA (polyvinyl acetate) glue is good for large areas. It is white but dries transparent. It can be used to thicken water-based paint. Protect clothing and wash brushes after use.

Wallpaper paste makes a good glue for large areas. For safety, use the non-fungicidal kind.

Tube glue should be non-toxic. Do not use instant-bond or solvent based glues.

Sticky tape. It is best to cut several lengths at once and attach lightly to a work surface edge for easy use.

Magnetic shapes are available from large stationers and shops stocking educational toys. They can often be bought as alphabet letters or numbers.

Felt-tip pens should be the non-permanent washable kind. Encourage children to replace the tops after use.

Glitter should be used with care. Avoid rubbing eyes during use and wash hands afterwards. Tip any excess into the fold of a magazine and pour back into the container.

Knives should be plastic, or round-ended kitchen knives.

Paintbrushes. Use small household paintbrushes for painting large areas. Use children's paintbrushes for finer patterns.